7 Chakras

A Guide to Understanding Your 7 Chakra Spiritual Power Centers, and How to Open, Balance, and Heal Them

by Simone LePage

Table of Contents

Introduction

Your chakras are your body's centers of energy. They allow life force to flow into and out of your being, and your health and life can be much improved when your chakras are strong, open, and balanced.

The main function of the chakras is to energize the physical body and help a person to develop self-consciousness. Chakras have a great effect on people's physical, emotional, mental and spiritual health. By learning about your seven power centers and how they work, you can learn how to regulate them for our own benefit.

For those who don't know much about the seven chakras and how they affect our bodies and lives, this book is for you. It will serve as an easy-to-understand guide for beginners, as well as a supplement for those who already have a general understanding. As you read through the chapters, you will discover what the seven chakras are, and the importance of keeping them open and balanced. You'll find information about the signs of blocked chakras, but most importantly, you'll learn how you can keep your chakras open and balanced at all times. If you're ready to start the holistic healing process in your life, let's get started!

Chapter 1:   What Are The Seven Chakras?

Chakra is a Sanskrit term that means "wheel." A lot of people hear about chakras in passing, possibly from health buffs and yoga practitioners, but most people really don't know what the word means. Simply put, chakras are energy centers in the body. There are seven chakras and each plays an essential role in a person's well-being.

Psychics see the chakras as wheels of energy that are constantly spinning. On the other hand, clairvoyants have a different perception of the seven energy centers, seeing them as colorful wheels or flowers. The locations of the seven chakras range from the base of the spine to the top of the head. The chakras have a fixed position in the spine, but work through the front and back of your body. One should also keep in mind that the seven chakras rotate and vibrate at varying speeds, with the first chakra rotating at the slowest speed and the seventh chakra rotating at the highest speed. Chakras also have different sizes and brightness, which vary depending upon a person's present physical, mental, spiritual and emotional condition. Certain colors affect the chakras, and gemstones are often used to stimulate a chakra for particular purposes. It's easy to remember the colors of the seven chakras, since they are also the colors of the rainbow.

If you are a beginner or are fairly new to the chakras, then you will find this chapter very useful. Here is a simple guide to the seven chakras – their locations, colors and what they represent.

The Root Chakra

Location: This energy center is found at the base of the spine, or the coccyx.

Color: Red

What It Represents: This chakra stands for foundation, stability and the feeling of being grounded. It also has something to do with how a person connects to the physical and material world.

Connected with the root chakra are issues concerning the basic survival needs, such as food, clothing, shelter, money, employment, and independence.

The Sacral Chakra

Location: This energy center is found at the lower abdomen, around the spleen or a couple of inches below the navel.

Color: Orange

What It Represents: This chakra stands for a person's ability to accept other people, as well as new experiences.

Connected with the sacral chakra are issues concerning pleasure, sexuality, well-being, and sense of abundance.

The Solar Plexus Chakra

Location: This energy center is found in the upper abdomen area.

Color: Yellow

What It Represents: This chakra stands for being in control of one's life, as well as confidence and self-empowerment. It also represents intelligence, wit and a sense of humor.

Connected with the solar plexus chakra are issues concerning self-esteem, self-image, self-confidence, self-worth and self-control.

The Heart Chakra

Location: This energy center is found right above the heart, at the center of the chest.

Color: Green

What It Represents: This chakra stands for a person's capability to love. This energy center is connected with emotions, particularly the ability to give and receive love.

Connected with the heart chakra are issues concerning inner peace, joy and love. It is also linked with compassion, forgiveness, platonic love and empathy.

The Throat Chakra

Location: This energy center is found at the front of the throat.

Color: Blue

What It Represents: This chakra stands for an individual's aptitude for communication.

Connected with the throat chakra are issues concerning truth and the ability to express oneself. It is somewhat linked to relationships and the person's ability to express himself openly to those for whom he cares. The throat chakra also covers a person's trust issues and capability to speak objectively and truthfully.

The Third Eye Chakra

Location: This energy center is found at the center of the forehead. Due to its location, the third eye chakra is also often referred to as the "brow chakra."

Color: Indigo

What It Represents: This chakra stands for the ability to stay focused, to see the whole picture, and to look beyond what's in front of us.

Connected with the third eye chakra are issues concerning imagination, intuition, wisdom and the decision-making process. It also covers emphatic skills, self-realization and the ability to learn from past mistakes and move forward with no emotional baggage.

The Crown Chakra

Location: This energy center is found at the crown of the scalp, or the very top of the head.

Color: Violet; but, in some traditions, this chakra has no color

What It Represents: This chakra stands for full spiritual connection.

Connected with the crown chakra are issues concerning the ability to connect spiritually, the attainment of real happiness and the possession of inner and outer beauty. It covers man's spiritual growth and development, as well as the connection of man to the universe and to a higher being.

Now that you have an idea about the location of the seven energy centers, the colors that can stimulate them and what each chakra represents, you can proceed to learn about signs that your chakras might be clogged or misaligned. The next chapter describes the consequences of having blocked and out-of-balance chakras.

Chapter 2: Ramifications of Blocked Or Out-Of-Balance Chakras

Chakras are the energy centers of the body, and it is through these centers that life energy flows. If one of an individual's seven chakras are blocked, or is not aligned, it could result in health problems. Therefore, everyone must have an understanding of each chakra and the things that we can do to make sure that our energy centers are always open and balanced.

When the chakras are open and aligned, a person will experience good health at all times and will feel a sense of well-being. And while the closing of the chakras should be avoided, they should also not be opened too wide because that can lead to massive amounts of energy flowing through the body. People whose chakras are closed or opened too widely are prone to illnesses and other problems.

Individuals that block out their negative experiences and refuse to deal with their emotions may very well be preventing the flow of natural energy in their body. When this occurs, the chakras are hindered from developing and maturing. In order to keep the chakras open, a person needs to embrace every experience and accept events happening in his or her life. If one fails to do so, it results in the chakras getting blocked or clogged, which prevents the chakras from spinning. The clockwise spinning motions of the chakras work to process the energies that flow in and out of the body. Balanced chakras result in general well-being. Therefore, blocked or misaligned chakras need to be fixed in order for a person to be healthy and happy.

Each of the seven energy centers of the body is strategically placed in a particular part of the body because it corresponds to specific physical ailments. The chakras are also the sources of people's emotional and mental strengths. Hence, when a person is sick or in pain, the emotional and mental behavior is also affected. Life energy should continuously flow in and out of the body and should not become stagnant, as this can cause a physical, emotional, spiritual, or mental malfunction.

It is crucial that the chakra mind-body balance be maintained. It clears the energy and brings about a healthy state of mind. Are you experiencing any physical ailment? Do you have unresolved emotions? Here are signs that your chakras might be blocked or out of balance:

Root Chakra Problems

• Physical Signs:

When the root chakra is blocked, misaligned, or out of balance, a person can experience problems in the areas near the tailbone, where it is located. The prostate gland, reproductive organs, tailbone, rectum, legs and feet are all connected to the root chakra. Common ailments related to the root chakra include constipation, indigestion, eating disorders, knee pain, arthritis, sciatica, anemia and chronic fatigue.

- Emotional Signs:

A person whose root chakra is out of balance can have problems feeling stable. He may feel that he is unable to take control of his life and can experience trouble with employment, housing and money. The root chakra may also have something to do with life-changing decisions such as changing homes, careers, or pursuing a different field.

When this chakra is open and balanced, a person feels grounded and stable.

Sacral Chakra Problems

- Physical Signs:

Reproductive issues and ailments concerning the bladder, kidney, pelvis and hips are connected to the sacral chakra. Sexual issues are also connected to the sacral chakra.

- Emotional Signs:

People whose sacral chakra is out of balance experience problems in their relationships. They are afraid to make commitments and express their feelings and emotions. There is also a fear of intimacy and the inability to have long-term relationships. The sacral chakra affects creativity, the ability to have fun, and a person's tendency toward addiction. When the sacral chakra is blocked, a person may have fears of betrayal and being impotent.

When this chakra is open and balanced, a person becomes outgoing, creative, passionate, sexual and willing to take risks.

Solar Plexus Chakra Problems

- Physical Signs:

When the solar plexus chakra is blocked or misaligned, the person may experience the following physical ailments: physical exhaustion, high blood

16

pressure, stomach ulcers and diseases concerning the pancreas, gallbladder, liver and colon.

- Emotional Signs:

The solar plexus chakra affects a person's self-esteem. Feelings of inadequacy, insecurities about one's physical appearance and fear of rejection or criticism are all connected with the solar plexus chakra.

When this chakra is open and balanced, a person feels happy and satisfied with himself. He feels assertive and has confidence.

Heart Chakra Problems

- Physical Signs:

An out-of-balance heart chakra results in ailments related to the lungs, breasts and respiratory and lymphatic systems. Wrist, shoulder, arm and upper back pains are also connected to the heart chakra.

- Emotional Signs:

Strong emotions, like depression, bitterness and anger, are signs that the heart chakra is blocked. A person may also feel emotional suffocation, jealousy and a fear of abandonment. Problems with romantic relationships and the inability to connect with another person on a deeper level are signs that the heart chakra is unhealthy.

A healthy heart chakra gives a person joy and the ability to trust, love, forgive, feel gratitude and show compassion.

Throat Chakra Problems

•   Physical Signs:

The usual conditions related to a blocked throat chakra include ear infections, thyroid and any throat problems, illnesses concerning parts of the face, and shoulder and neck pain.

•   Emotional Signs:

Problems with the throat chakra manifest themselves through a person's inability to communicate, or freely express his thoughts, ideas and emotions using verbal, written, or body language. There are also problems related to speaking truthfully and objectively.

A person who has a balanced throat chakra will enjoy the ability of communicating well with other people. Speaking and listening are never a problem, and it is also easy to speak truthfully, honestly and fairly.

Third Eye Chakra Problems

- Physical Signs:

People that suffer from vision problems, sinus issues, constant headaches, hearing loss, or hormone imbalances may very well have a blocked third eye chakra. Also, when this chakra is misaligned, flu-like symptoms, such as fever, muscle aches and swollen glands, can be experienced by the person.

- Emotional Signs:

The third eye chakra has much to do with an individual's ability to learn from past experiences and look forward to the future. A person who has a blocked chakra may be unable to let go of painful past experiences, or to move on and learn from these.

19

A clear and balanced third eye chakra allows people to feel empathy and develop psychic abilities. These people are more focused on their goals and have a good grasp of reality.

Crown Chakra Problems

•   Physical Signs:

An imbalanced crown chakra can result in hypersensitivity to light and sound. It also results in extreme feelings of loneliness and an inability to learn. A person with an imbalanced crown chakra can suffer from migraines, mental disorders and ailments related to the eye.

•   Emotional Signs:

When the crown chakra is not open and aligned, the individual may have problems accepting the presence of a greater power. He is also unable to realize his part in the bigger scheme of things and can be very close-minded about religion or spirituality. It is also common for folks that have an unhealthy crown chakra to feel alienated and have prejudices.

By this time, you may already have realized the importance of keeping the chakras open and balanced. If any of the seven chakras is blocked or misaligned, the body may experience certain physical ailments and negative emotional conditions. In the next chapter, you will learn how you can keep all of your chakras open, aligned and balanced.

Chapter 3: Opening, Balancing, and Healing Your Chakras

Luckily, there are ways to keep the seven chakras all in good health. With open and balanced energy centers, life energy can flow freely and naturally within and through your body. For those who are new to the chakras, you can always get in touch with a trained energy medicine practitioner to check the condition of your chakras. This expert can help you to get your chakras functioning properly. Nevertheless, here are some things that can help you maintain open and balanced chakras:

The Use of Gemstones and Crystals

Gemstones and crystals are very helpful in keeping the chakras balanced and open. They respond to the life energy that courses in and out of the body and send out electrical vibrations to free or clear the clogged chakras. All of the chakras are associated with specific colors, so to help keep a chakra healthy, just use stones or crystals of the color associated with that chakra. For example, green crystals or gemstones can be worn to balance the heart chakra, and red stones can help open or align the root chakra.

Eat the Right Foods

Certain foods have been known to fuel the chakras. You just have to know what specific foods can help each of your power centers. For example, root vegetables, protein-rich foods and spices are good for the root chakra. Sweet fruits, honey and nuts are great for the sacral chakra, while grains and dairy are good for your solar plexus chakra. For the heart chakra, leafy greens and tea are recommended. Placate your throat chakra with a lot of fruits, especially citrus fruits. Feed your third eye chakra with red wine and dark blue fruits, such as blueberries, grapes and raspberries. However, the crown chakra can benefit from some abstinence, or fasting.

Chakra Balancing Baths

This is a kind of meditation that will help clear and balance the seven chakras. It involves sitting comfortably and visualizing colored lights moving throughout the body.

Clean Your Chakras

Believe it or not, the conditions of your chakras are often mirrored in your home. Are most of your rooms disarrayed? Is there too much clutter? Cleaning up and getting rid of clutter can do wonders for your energy centers. There are also specific areas or parts of your home that correspond with each chakra. For example, the basement for the root chakra, the master bedroom for the sacral chakra, the comfort rooms and bathrooms for the solar plexus chakra, the kitchen and dining room for the heart chakra, the family room for the throat chakra, the home office, windows and den for the third eye chakra, and the attic and rain gutters for the crown chakra. Clean your home daily and your chakras will stay open and balanced.

Exercises to Balance the Chakra

Physical activities such as hula hooping, belly dancing, marching and stretching are proven to help get the chakras properly and optimally functioning. For the root chakra, it helps to march and do squats. The sacral chakra can benefit from pelvic thrusts and circular motions, while the solar plexus chakra can be balanced by belly dancing exercises and hula hooping. Swimming and hugging are great for the heart chakra, and visualization exercises are beneficial for the third eye chakra. The crown chakra can be opened and balanced by meditating.

Incantations to Balance the Chakras

You can help to balance and align your chakras through a combination of incantations and breathing exercises. Repeating these incantations a number of times, coupled with a rhythmic inhaling and exhaling, can help center your chakras.

Playing the Drums to Activate the Heart Chakra

Drum players have an advantage as the heart chakra is stimulated by the rhythm of drums. But you too can play the drums to balance the heart chakra.

There are actually many more methods that anyone can try to help the chakras. Yoga, a form of meditative exercise, is one of the most popular. Aromatherapy, visualization, meditation, acupuncture, massage, exercise and heat are also effective ways to keep the chakras balanced.

Chapter 4: Understanding What Causes The Chakras To Be Blocked

Chakras serve as the body's energy centers, and it is through these centers that the life energy can course through the body. When the chakras are open and balanced, the person is in an excellent physical, emotional and mental state. However, when these energy centers are blocked, misaligned, or unbalanced, physical, emotional, spiritual and mental issues can manifest. So what causes the chakras to become blocked and out of balance?

As we go through life, we encounter various situations and people, and gain all kinds of experiences. There are bad ones that make us sad, disappointed and change our lives for the worse, but there are also good experiences that teach us lessons, help us grow and enrich our lives. How we handle these experiences can affect our health and, ultimately, our lives.

Chakras can become blocked, clogged, misaligned, and out of balance when we choose not to face or let go of painful past experiences. People that live in denial and refuse to accept their experiences can suffer from numerous ailments. When we bury bad memories instead of releasing them, or hold on to anger and keep grudges, our chakras become blocked.

Therefore, it is very important to face our life experiences. Painful memories need to be accepted, not buried. It is easier to forgive than to hold on to anger or plot for revenge. The energy that it takes to keep and sustain these negative feelings, emotions and thoughts is so great that it can harm the body and mind. Accept situations as they happen in your life. Stop trying to fight or change things that you cannot. Accept the things that you cannot control. You don't need to be in control of everything, and you must accept this too. In doing so, you allow the life energy to flow freely in your body.

One or all of the chakras can shut down. When only one or two of these energy centers are blocked or misaligned, the other chakras will try to compensate and can become overworked. This destroys the balance between the seven chakras and can be the cause of minor and major diseases in the body. Any negative energy in the body, such as guilt, denial, anger, jealousy, repression, as well as other negative emotions, can block the chakras. Therefore, it is always advisable to let go of any negative memories, experiences, emotions and thoughts. Don't let these prevent new energy from flowing into your body.

Acceptance and forgiveness are among the best ways to keep the chakras open. Release any negative energy from your body by accepting the way things are in your life, and by forgiving those that have wronged you. Once you accept and forgive, a great burden will be lifted from your shoulders, and this will do wonders for your health and happiness.

Chapter 5: Affirmations To Strengthen Your Chakras

The power of affirmations may have originated with the universal belief in the power of words. Words are powerful and, when uttered or released into the universe, affect the forces out there, causing whatever was said to become a reality. Affirmations are positive words that people repeat in order to make them happen. These words that are said over and over again can become a person's belief, and this belief can very well become a reality. Affirmations help people overcome negative thoughts and emotions, which help them, instead, to focus on the brighter side of things.

Chakras are blocked because of negative energies. Affirmations are used to keep the positive energies flowing and to get rid of the negative energies. The beauty of affirmations is that we can create them ourselves. We can have daily, weekly, monthly and yearly affirmations. Affirmations can be made for specific purposes, too. We can create affirmations for healing, balancing and opening our chakras. Try to make your own chakra affirmations and repeat the words out loud in order to help keep your chakras open and balanced. Here are samples of affirmations that help strengthen the seven chakras:

Affirmation for the Root Chakra

"I am in control of my life. I am where I want to be. I have all the things I need at this moment. Money is not my concern. I love my job."

Affirmation for the Sacral Chakra

"I am a sexual person. I welcome intimacy and want to make real commitments with the people I love. I will have a happy, fruitful and long-lasting relationship with that special person."

Affirmation for the Solar Plexus Chakra

"I am confident with my looks and my abilities. I am happy with my appearance. I accept my body for what it is. I am beautiful / handsome."

Affirmation for the Heart Chakra

"I am loved and I am capable of love. I will remove anger, jealousy, resentment, envy, greed and other negative emotions from my heart."

Affirmation for the Throat Chakra

"I have a voice and I will express how I feel truthfully and without fear of judgment. I will use my words to bridge gaps and to be productive."

Affirmation for the Third Eye Chakra

"I accept all experiences and learn from them. I will let go of bad memories and look forward to better possibilities. My goals are realistic and I will achieve them."

Affirmation for the Crown Chakra

"I know that there is a higher power and that I have a part to play in the Universe. I am flexible and open-minded. I will remove all of my prejudices."

Repeat your affirmations many times in a day. You can say them a dozen times or a hundred times. The more you say your affirmations, the more positive you'll feel. Whenever you feel down or blue, just repeat your affirmations and you'll drive away the negative energy coursing through your body. Focus on the positive all the time and let the positive energies flow into your energy centers.

Conclusion

Learning about the chakras, or the seven power centers in the body, can be very beneficial. People can attain happiness and good health when the chakras are aligned and open. Although many people are aware of holistic healing and how the chakras work, many people hear the word "chakra," and immediately think about yoga and the spiritual beliefs of India; but that is all that they know about it. It is, therefore, both unfortunate and sad that knowledge about the seven chakras is limited to only a small number of people. If only more people knew about these energy centers, then more people could be healthier and happier with their lives.

People experience physical ailments and spiritual and emotional issues, but some have no idea that the cause of these could be a blocked or misaligned chakra. Just imagine if chakra healing became common knowledge and all people were aware of balancing the chakras.

With an open mind, and through following the information presented in this book, you can understand how each chakra works, its role in your physical, emotional, mental and spiritual health, and how you can open and heal them for improved wellbeing.

Finally, I'd like to thank you for purchasing this book! If you enjoyed it or found it helpful, I'd greatly appreciate it if you'd take a moment to leave a review on Amazon. Thank you!

27565677R00031

Printed in Great Britain
by Amazon